I0883591

NORTH-WEST HALF-CAB BUSES

THE TWILIGHT YEARS

MIKE RHODES

AMBERLEY

First published 2024

Amberley Publishing
The Hill, Stroud
Gloucestershire, GL5 4EP

www.amberley-books.com

Copyright © Mike Rhodes, 2024

The right of Mike Rhodes to be identified as the Author of this work has been asserted in accordance with the Copyrights, Designs and Patents Act 1988.

ISBN 978 1 3981 1863 8 (print)
ISBN 978 1 3981 1864 5 (ebook)

All rights reserved. No part of this book may be reprinted or reproduced or utilised in any form or by any electronic, mechanical or other means, now known or hereafter invented, including photocopying and recording, or in any information storage or retrieval system, without the permission in writing from the Publishers.

British Library Cataloguing in Publication Data.
A catalogue record for this book is available from the British Library.

Typesetting by SJmagic DESIGN SERVICES, India.
Printed in the UK.

Introduction

North-West England is a compact area and in its day provided much of the industrial manufacturing output of the country. Many of the towns had their own transport systems and these provided the necessary means for workers to get to and from the factories. As the nation became more independent during the 1960s the use of public transport began to dwindle and what were known as 'Works Specials' started to decline. It was the same with regards to 'Football Specials'. The Football League was founded with teams from the North West and the Midlands; nowhere else in the country was there such a concentration of league teams as in the North West. Supporters of the likes of Blackburn Rovers, Chester City, Everton, Liverpool, Manchester City, Manchester United, Oldham Athletic, Preston North End and Rochdale all relied heavily on their local corporation buses to get them to the match. The common theme was that it was generally the oldest buses in the fleet which were used on such specials – the half-cabs.

By the 1970s such specials were few in number, but the half-cab bus was still present in all the major bus fleets in the area. The two Passenger Transport Executives (PTEs) based in the North West, Manchester (SELNEC/GMPTE) and Merseyside (MPTE), absorbed seventeen former municipal bus fleets between them and consequentially ended up with a motley collection of different bus types. Many of these represented the local bus builders of the time with regards to the chassis and the body choice. Leyland Motors, not unsurprisingly, dominated the local market, but there were also examples of the less-profuse Crossley and Foden types to be found. The more well-known bodybuilders located in the region were Burlingham of Blackpool, East Lancashire Coachbuilders of Blackburn, Leyland Motors and Massey Brothers and Northern Counties, both of which had their factories in Wigan. Buses built by these concerns were well represented throughout the region.

That is not to say that the local operators didn't buy their products from elsewhere, because they did. Accrington (Hyndburn), Blackburn, Chester and Lancashire United (LUT) had an affinity with the Guy Arab chassis, whilst Liverpool, Morecambe, Rochdale and St Helens amassed sizeable fleets of AEC Regents. Manchester Corporation tended to alternate between Daimler and Leyland products when placing their chassis orders, whilst near neighbour Salford also had some Daimlers in its fleet. With regards to bodywork, the Midlands-based Metro-Cammell Carriage & Wagon Works (MCCW) was a popular choice with Bolton, Manchester, Preston, Salford and St Helens. Both Blackburn and Wigan were staunchly loyal to their local bodybuilders, with Wigan in particular dividing its orders equally between the two local concerns. Half-cab bus bodies ceased to be built for the home market at the end of the 1960s, with Stockport Corporation taking some of the last in the form of six Leyland PD3s with forward-entrance East Lancs bodies in February 1969.

As with many bus fleets throughout the country, the double-decker bus far outweighed the single-decker in number. Burnley Colne & Nelson (BCN) was one operator that bucked the trend. BCN had an operating agreement with Ribble Motors and many of the routes in the surrounding area were jointly operated. These took buses of both operators along a number of East Lancashire's country roads where double-deck buses would have been unsuitable. Whereas Ribble operated various types of single-deckers over the years, ranging from Leyland Tigers to Bristol REs and Leyland Nationals, BCN tended to favour East Lancs-bodied Leyland Tigers and Tiger Cubs, the former with a half-cab configuration. The Tigers lasted in service until August 1976 and were some of the last of the configuration to be used in the country. Of a lesser significance, Preston retained two similar Leyland Tigers until 1968, one of which was later used as a mobile polling booth and a towing vehicle, and likewise with Rossendale who also retained a Leyland Tiger beyond its operating life for use as a towing vehicle.

Blackburn Corporation had bought two small batches of Crossley-bodied Leyland Tigers in 1947/8 and for many years they worked the hilly routes to Revidge, which climbed the steep grades on either side of Corporation Park (denoted as East and West). These lasted in service until the late 1960s. Three of Ribble Motor's half-cab Leyland Tigers had a prolonged life when Southport Corporation bought them in 1963 and converted then to open-top buses for use on tours and the Promenade service. These lasted long enough to pass with the undertaking to the MPTE and were repainted into Verona green and cream. They were eventually taken out of service in the mid-1970s. Finally, City of Lancaster kept a former Lancaster City Transport (LCT) Northern Counties-bodied Daimler CVG5 in the fleet for special occasions; it was one of three purchased in 1952.

As bus companies turned to buses that were suitable for One Man Operation (OPO), the conventional double-decker bus began to disappear. Salford and Stockport had taken deliveries of the type as late as the end of the 1960s, and not surprisingly these were some of the last to operate for Greater Manchester PTE (formerly SELNEC). Similarly, St Helens remained true to the type, and again these were some of the last to operate for the MPTE – the PTEs withdrew their last half-cabs from normal service in 1981 and 1979 respectively. It was a similar situation with the municipal fleets: only Blackpool continued to use the type beyond 1982, with the last PD3s not being withdrawn until 1988. Blackpool, Burnley and GM Buses (successor to the PTE) all later dabbled with second-hand London Routemasters, variously between 1986 and 1994.

The other major fleets in the area were Crosville, Lancashire United Transport (LUT), North Western Roadcar and Ribble Motors. The former's buses could be seen mainly in Chester, Liverpool and Warrington and various towns and villages in between. Their half-cab buses were all of the Bristol Lodekka family, which were invariably bodied by Eastern Coach Works. LUT operated out of three garages in south Lancashire and their buses could be seen in some numbers in Atherton, Bolton, Farnworth, Leigh, Salford, Swinton and Wigan. LUT operated a large fleet of Northern Counties-bodied Guy

Arabs, the last of which succumbed to the scrap man at the end of 1980. Also, LUT had become part of the Greater Manchester PTE fleet on 1 January 1976, but continued to be run as a separate company until 1 April 1981. Part of the North-Western fleet was also absorbed by SELNEC on 1 January 1972, with a number of AEC Renowns and Dennis Lolines transferring over. At the same time the ownership of buses of the same two types based at three garages located in Cheshire were transferred over to Crosville.

Ribble Motors operated a vast fleet of over 1,200 buses and coaches; the Ribble empire stretched from Carlisle in the far north to the Lancashire/Cheshire boundary in the south. Over the post-war years various types of half-cab buses had been operated, including many of Leyland's Titan range of PD1s, PD2s and PD3s. Whereas virtually all the PD3 types operated had full fronted bodywork, the last batches of PD2s received in the mid-1950s had half-cab-style bodies built by Burlingham and Metro-Cammell. The last of these in normal service worked out of Bootle garage on Merseyside and were withdrawn in 1972. A handful of both types were used as driver tuition vehicles for a few more years, with PD2/13 No. 1399 (TU3) still being noted in use at Skelmersdale garage in 1981.

There were a number of small independent operators in the region. Four worthy of special note are Holmeswood Coaches of Rufford, Lonsdale Coaches of Heysham, J. Fishwick & Sons of Leyland and A. Mayne & Son of Manchester. Holmeswood was established in 1947 and was still operating in 2022. Besides the coaching arm of the business, the operator had always been involved in school contract work and obtained a number of cast-off half-cab buses in the 1970s to operate these. At the same time, Lonsdale also obtained cast-off buses from other operators, but for a much different reason. The operator had a long-standing contract with Taylor Woodrow, who was engaged on the construction of the two Heysham nuclear power stations, to convey workers to and from the site to various destinations in the county. The buses involved were generally painted a distinctive sulphur yellow. Whether this was supposed to symbolise a connection with the nuclear industry or otherwise is not known. The coaching side of the business was acquired by City of Lancaster Transport in 1988, whilst the bus operations ceased on completion of the construction works in the mid-1980s.

One of the more significant independent operators in the region was J. Fishwick & Sons, who were based in Leyland – home of the original Leyland Motors factory. Fishwick ran buses in the Leyland and Preston localities from the early twentieth century until 24 October 2015, when the company was placed in administration; not surprisingly they had a strong affinity for Leyland products, with a selection of PD1s and PD2s amongst their ranks. Virtually all of their half-cabs carried lowbridge bodies on account of the low bridge that carried the Preston to Southport railway line over Leyland Road at Penwortham. The bridge was removed in 1970 – six years after the line to Southport was closed. Fishwick even had their own bus station in Preston which was situated in Fox Street; it closed in October 1969 when all the operator's services were transferred to the new central bus station.

Finally, A. Mayne & Son Ltd was a small family-run bus and coach operator established in 1920 that co-existed with its much larger Manchester neighbour for many years until the firm was eventually taken over by GM Buses in January 2008. Their principal routes ran out of Manchester city centre and along Ashton New Road (where the garage was situated). Amongst the ranks of buses operated in the 1960s and 1970s was a small number of AEC Regent Vs that had been obtained new between 1957 and 1965. These contrasted markedly with the Daimlers and Leylands operated by the GMPTE. Over the years they could frequently be seen on service 213 (formerly 46), which ran from Manchester's Stevenson Square to Droylesden. The coaching arm of the business was still functioning in 2022.

So, as previously stated in a companion volume, the only way to sample these types of buses now is by visiting one of the many bus preservation sites throughout the country, or more particularly those that are situated in the North West. These include the Museum of Transport in Greater Manchester, based in part of a former Manchester Corporation bus garage; the North West Museum of Road Transport, which is also based in a former bus/trolleybus garage in St Helens; and the British Commercial Vehicle Museum, which is aptly situated in Leyland. Also very active in the region are the Merseyside Transport Trust, which is located near Burscough, and the Ribble Vehicle Preservation Trust, both of whom organise a number of running days throughout the year. A variety of half-cab buses can always be found at these institutions and events.

All the pictures in this book were taken by the author, who retains copyright.

Mike Rhodes

Accrington Corporation was renamed Hyndburn Borough Transport on 1 April 1974. The authority had latterly bought small numbers of Guy Arabs and Leyland Titans before beginning a long association with the Atlantean in 1969. Parked in the garage yard on 20 July 1976 were Guy Arab V No. 165 and PD3As Nos 159/66/8/9 along with Tiger Cubs Nos 21/2/4.

Numbers 158/9 were East Lancs-bodied (ELC) Leyland PD3A/1s, which joined the fleet in 1962 along with Tiger Cubs Nos 17/8. They were seen parked together in the garage yard on 15 October 1977.

In 1964 the Corporation purchased three Guy Arab Vs; two had East Lancs bodies whilst the third was bodied by the East Lancashire firm's subsidiary works at Neepsend in Sheffield. Number 164 was one of the former and was photographed in the town's Peel Street bus station on 3 August 1974 with a local service to Oswaldtwistle.

The operator's intake of new buses in 1958 consisted of two Guy Arab IVs and two Leyland PD2/31s, all of which were bodied by East Lancs. One of the latter, No. 149 is seen at Peel Street waiting to depart for nearby Clayton-le-Moors on 25 August 1975. Peel Street bus station was closed in 2016 and was replaced by a bus interchange closer to the railway station.

Not unnaturally, many of Blackburn Corporation's buses carried bodies built by the town's own East Lancashire Coachbuilders (ELC). No. 151 (renumbered from No. 140) was one of ten ELC-bodied Guy Arab IVs that joined the fleet in 1957. It is pictured at Intack on 3 August 1974.

On the same day these four Guy Arabs were also on the depot. Whilst Nos 147 and 158 (previously numbered 141) are from the same batch, Nos 160/4 were new in 1961 and have the so-called 'Johannesburg' radiator cowl, which was synonymous with that city's Guy Arabs of the same period. The olive green and cream suited the buses.

ELC-bodied Leyland PD2A/24 No. 28 was displaying a revised livery layout when photographed in Accrington's Peel Street bus station on 25 August 1975. The undertaking bought two batches of twelve PD2As in 1962 and 1964. The next buses to join the fleet were a batch of eight Leyland Tiger Cubs in 1967.

Following the amalgamation of the Blackburn and Darwen municipal bus fleets on 1 April 1974 the livery was changed again to a red roof with white in between and dark green to the lower bodywork. Guy Arab No. 161 was photographed at the Boulevard on 3 August 1974.

Also seen at the Boulevard on 3 August 1974 was 1964 ELC-bodied Leyland PD2A/24 No. 34. Note the style of destination display, which was favoured by only a small number of operators. This was the last Blackburn half-cab bus in use and was withdrawn after service on 7 March 1981.

Bridge Street, alongside the railway, was used as a layover point for out of service buses and was also the departure point for the special buses to Ewood Park on match days. Leyland Titan No. 41 displays the revised combined livery and is seen parked in Bridge Street on 29 March 1980.

Following the Second World War the municipality replaced its ageing fleet with both Leyland and Guy double-deckers between 1946 and 1949. No. 118 was a Leyland-bodied PD1A which had entered service in 1948. On 12 September 1976 it was resting in Geoff Lister's (dealer) yard in Bolton somewhat the worse for wear.

New in 1961, ELC-bodied Guy Arab IV No. 160 was parked in the yard at Intack on 20 July 1976. The depot site was still in use by the Blackburn Bus Company (Transdev) in 2023, although new maintenance facilities had replaced the old garage buildings.

A busy scene at the Boulevard on 17 June 1977 sees Leyland Titan No. 22 departing for the local district of Feniscowles via Ewood. Nine other buses are partially visible all of which are painted in the new livery. The Boulevard, for so long a focal point of both the local corporation's and Ribble Motors' services, was closed in 2013 and replaced by a new bus station nearby.

Titan No. 37 was photographed in Blackburn Road at Darwen on 25 September 1976. To the left is the entrance to the former Darwen Corporation garage with two former corporation buses just visible.

Blackburn Corporation bought five Crossley-bodied Leyland PS1s in 1947 with another five joining the fleet the following year. For many years they were principally used on the East and West routes, which climbed the steep gradients either side of Corporation Park. Now sold, out of service No. 8 is seen in use with KME Manufacturing & Engineering Co. and is parked at their works on Kirkby Industrial Estate on Merseyside on 19 March 1976.

Following the cessation of the Second World War Blackburn began a long-standing practice of buying Guys and Leylands for their double-deck bus requirements. No. 122 was one of a batch of twenty Crossley-bodied Guy Arab IIIs which joined the fleet in 1949. This one was retained for driver training duties and was photographed at Intack on 3 August 1974. Similar bus No. 133 is now preserved.

The three main Lancashire seaside towns all operated open-top buses, although Blackpool also had a sizeable number of open-top trams. Long after the buses had gone Blackpool acquired this 1967 ELC-bodied Leyland PD2A/30 from Eastbourne (see inset) in 1989. It was numbered 532 and painted in a version of the Routemaster livery. It was photographed at Gynn Square on 8 September 1991; it was retired from service in 1999.

For many years Blackpool Corporation purchased double-deck buses with fully enclosed fronts, exemplified by the 100 Burlingham-bodied Leyland PD2/5s bought by the municipality between 1949 and 1951. After several decades the first half-cab buses to join the fleet were twenty MCCW-bodied Leyland PD3A/1s in 1965. Number 392 is depicted in Market Street on 13 September 1979.

Number 398 was photographed at the Halfway House terminus of route 5 in Squires Gate Lane on 26 September 1981. At this time the route also worked round the district in the opposite direction as service 5A. Services 5/5A ran via the town centre to the Grange Park estate. This Titan was withdrawn a few weeks later.

In the early 1980s the operator added more green to the livery layout on the PD3A repaints, whereas previously green had only been applied to the mudguards. Number 399 has paused at Talbot Square on 23 July 1983 on a service 22 journey from Halfway House to Cleveleys. Numbers 390/4/9 were the last three of the batch in service, all being withdrawn later in the year.

Blackpool Corporation's buses could be seen throughout a large swathe of the Fylde Coast from Fleetwood in the north to Lytham in the south-east. Another of the 1965 batch of PD3As, No. 390, is seen crossing the Preston to Blackpool railway line at Carleton on 11 July 1978 on the long service 14 to Fleetwood. Number 390 lasted in service until 1983 and is now preserved.

Seen at the same location but travelling in the opposite direction on 13 March 1977 is No. 529, which was new in 1968. Note that the crossing gates had been replaced by lifting barriers in the intervening fifteen months. Carleton signal box was closed on 10 November 2017 at the start of the electrification works of the line. By coincidence No. 529 is also preserved.

In 1967/8 Blackpool added a further forty rear-entrance PD3As to its fleet, all of which were again bodied by MCCW. No. 519 is seen in Common Edge Road on 26 September 1980 on service 11C from Talbot Road bus station to St Annes. Service 11C ran from 1940 until 1994.

Another of the same batch, No. 521, was photographed outside Yates's Wine Lodge in Talbot Road on 29 May 1977 on its way from Victoria Hospital to South Pier. The Lodge was badly damaged by fire in February 2009 and subsequently demolished. The site has since been redeveloped.

Number 538 was one of the last PD3As taken into stock by Blackpool Corporation in 1968 and was one of the last nine in service twenty years later. It is seen in the revised colour scheme at the Halfway House terminus of service 5A to Grange Park on 16 January 1986.

Number 507 was selected to carry this special centenary livery which was later applied to the acquired Routemasters and the former Eastbourne PD2A. It was photographed at the Fleetwood terminus of service 14 on 14 July 1985. It is standing next to the site of the long-closed Fleetwood railway station. Number 507 was retained for service until 1995 and latterly used on service 12 alongside the Routemasters.

Even as late as 1980 the operator was still using a substantial number of back-loaders as testified by this impressive line-up recorded in the garage yard on 11 May. Only the lead two buses, Nos 504/5, can be identified. The last in the line has training bus markings below the upper-deck windows.

Blackpool trialled its first Routemaster in January 1986 when ex-LT RM1583 (later No. 521) paid a visit to the resort. Five more followed later in the year and a further six in 1988, with one more in 1989. Number 522 had been RM848 in the London Transport fleet. It is seen with competing Fylde Borough Atlantean No. 50 at Gynn Square on 20 August 1991, both of which are on services that served the Pontins Holiday Camp.

The Routemasters were also used on service 12 on which conductors had been retained. Number 525 (ex-LT RM1650) was photographed in Clifton Drive North in St Annes on 25 July 1987. The Routemasters were sold on to Reading Mainline in January 1997, although RM1650 returned to London and worked the two heritage routes from June 2008 to May 2013. It was recorded as being with a private owner in Redruth in Cornwall in April 2021.

On 16 June 1990 Nos 524 (ex-LT RM1640) and 523 (ex-LT RM1627) were waiting for custom at the Pontins Holiday Camp at Squires Gate. These two followed a similar path as RM1650 after departing Blackpool in 1997 with RM1640 reported as undergoing refurbishment in August 2015 and RM1627 residing with Dualway Coaches in Eire in June 2019.

Number 530 (ex-LT RM1989) was one of the second batch of six Routemasters that were acquired in April 1988. It was photographed opposite the Metropole Hotel on 18 July 1989 heading for the Pleasure Beach. The original 'Beachcomer' route was numbered 55 and ran from Starr Gate to Gynn Square.

Burnley, Colne & Nelson JOC (BCN) mainly favoured Leyland buses for both their double- and single-deck requirements. In 1959/61 the operator added a small batch of six East Lancs-bodied Leyland PD3/6s to the fleet, all of which were sold on to City of Lancaster in 1974. The former Burnley & Pendle (previously BCN) No. 236 (CoL No. 536) is seen in Damside bus station at Lancaster not long after acquisition on 10 August 1974. A Ribble MCCW-bodied Leyland PD3/5 can be seen in the background.

Between 1962 and 1967 BCN took stock of twenty-six Leyland PD2A/27s, which were variously bodied by either East Lancs or Northern Counties. Number 255 was new in 1965 and carried a Northern Counties-built body. It is seen in the company of ELC-bodied Leyland Tiger Cub No. 72 in Burnley bus station on 3 August 1974. It was withdrawn in 1978.

In 1954 BCN took stock of eleven rear-entrance ELC-bodied Leyland PS2/14 Tigers, adding another three the following year. In 1957–59 all of the batch were rebuilt as front-entrance buses by East Lancs. The last of these remained in service until 1976 and were possibly the last half-cab single-deck buses in service with any UK municipal bus operator. Number 44 is seen in Abingdon Road in Padiham on the last day of service, 29 August. At least five of the type – Nos 36/7, 40/1/5 – are thought to still exist in preservation in 2022.

Numbers 47–49 were received in early 1955 and two of the trio, Nos 48/9, are seen in the garage yard at Queensgate on 3 August 1974. These three were also rebuilt as forward-entrance buses but were withdrawn in 1974 and eventually scrapped.

On 6 July 1976, PS2 No. 45 had made the 24-mile trip to Preston on driver training duty. It is seen parked at the back of Preston bus station on layover. Borough of Preston Leyland Titan PD3s Nos 2 and 14 can also be seen parked out of service. This side of the bus station is no longer used by buses and has been pedestrianised.

The first batch of Leyland PD2A/27 half-cabs was received in 1962 and comprised Nos 238–41. First of the quartet, No. 238, is seen alongside 1954 ELC-bodied Leyland Tiger No. 46 over the pits inside the Queensgate garage on 3 August 1974.

On 25 August 1975 Nos 257 and 258 were parked in the garage yard. The former was the last of a batch of ten purchased in 1965, whilst the latter was the first of six more received in 1967. Despite the similar appearance, No. 257 was bodied by Northern Counties, whilst No. 258 had an East Lancs-built body. Note the BCN lettering below the front destination screens.

Repainted in the revised Burnley & Pendle fleet colours, ELC-bodied Leyland PD2A/27 No. 261 was photographed resting at the back of Burnley bus station on 20 August 1977; it lasted in service until 1980.

Burnley & Pendle followed Blackpool's example and purchased five redundant Routemasters in 1988. These were principally used on the 'Mainline' service to Colne. Number 187 *Dot Cotton* (ex-LT RM2087) was photographed in the garage yard on 25 November 1990. It was sold to Geoff Lister (dealer) in May 1992 and subsequently exported to Hungary.

Chester City Transport initially turned to Daimler and Foden for its double-deck bus requirements after the Second World War before obtaining three Massey-bodied Guy Arab IVs in 1953. These set the trend for the next sixteen years. Numbers 4–6 followed in 1954 and received Park Royal bodies. The first of the trio is seen in the garage yard, with a heavy covering of frost, on 24 January 1976.

Further Guy Arab IVs, fleet numbers 7–23, all with Massey-built bodies, joined the fleet between 1954 and 1957. These were all rear-entrance buses, with the next batch, Nos 24–26, being fitted with front entrances. On 9 February 1975, No. 21 was parked in the garage yard with the back of No. 7 also just visible. Number 21 was withdrawn later that year. General station was located at the front of the garage. Chester Northgate station was opened by the Cheshire Lines Committee (CLC) and closed on 6 October 1969.

Number 31 was one of four Guy Arab Vs obtained in 1963. A forward-entrance half-cab, it was again bodied by Massey Brothers of Wigan (Pemberton). It was photographed in Northgate Street in the city centre on 24 January 1976 on local service 2K to Auckland Road. It was taken out of service in early 1978 following the receipt of a batch of five new Leyland Fleetlines.

Chester's famous Eastgate Arch is the setting for this picture of Guy Arabs Nos 29 and 43 as seen on 24 January 1976. The former is a Mark IV model that was new in 1962, whilst the latter is a Mark V that joined the fleet in 1969 and was bodied by Northern Counties, Massey having ceased building bodywork for buses in 1967.

As can be seen here and in the previous picture, the operator changed the layout of the livery whilst still retaining the same colours. Number 36 was one of a batch of four Guy Arab Vs that joined the fleet in 1965. It was photographed in St Werburgh Street on 2 September 1981. The last half-cab in the fleet was No. 42, which lasted until 1982. The district of Saltney lies about 2½ miles to the west of Chester.

Darwen Corporation assembled a somewhat varied collection of buses after the Second World War, which included Crossleys and Leylands. Number 17 in the Darwen fleet was a one-off and was badged as a Crossley Regent V. It was fitted with an East Lancs doored rear-entrance body. It is seen at the Darwen Cemetery terminus on 25 September 1976. It was renumbered to 20 in the joint fleet and is now preserved.

The following year the municipality added three ELC-bodied Leyland PD2/31s to its fleet. These also had rear entrances fitted with doors. No. (1)25 was parked alongside Blackburn Guy Arab IV No. 161 (renumbered from 144) in the garage yard at Intack on 12 May 1975.

In 1964 the municipal operator added two ELC-bodied Leyland PD3A/1s to its fleet followed by two more in 1965. Darwen Corporation was merged with Blackburn Corporation on 1 April 1974 and the former Titan PD3 No. 27 is seen at Darwen Circus on 25 September 1976 with Blackburn Guy No. 169 in the background.

The former Darwen Corporation No. 31 was one of a second batch of three ELC-bodied Leyland PD3A/1s purchased in 1965. Looking immaculate, it is again seen on 25 September 1976 outside Blackburn railway station. The previously joint service between Blackburn and Darwen Cemetery had superseded the principal Darwen tram service.

On 3 August 1974 ELC-bodied Leyland PD3A/1 No. (1)32 was photographed in Darwen bus station with a departure for the local destination of Pothouse. Darwen buses never showed any route service numbers.

After their flirtation with seventy-two-seat PD3As, Darwen Corporation then bought batches of the smaller sixty-five-seat fibreglass-fronted PD2s between 1966 and 1969. Number (1)36 was new in 1967 and is seen in the new combined-authority livery in Darwen bus station on 16 April 1976.

The original Darwen tram depot was enlarged in the late 1930s to accommodate the growing number of buses in the fleet. The depot remained in use for a number of years after the merger with Blackburn. Seen inside on 16 April 1976 were from the left Leyland PD2A/27 No. 133, PD2/47s Nos 137/42 and 1972 Bristol RE No. 4, all of which were bodied by East Lancs.

After purchasing six Leyland-bodied PD1s in 1946, Lytham St Annes Corporation then bought six PD2/1s in 1948 and five PD2/12s in 1951. Number 10 was the first of the 1948 PD2/1s and passed to the newly formed Fylde Borough Transport on 1 April 1974. It is seen in use as a driver trainer at Preston bus station on 19 September 1974.

In 1960 Lytham Corporation acquired two Alexander-bodied Leyland PD1s from Warrington Corporation. Number 24 had been new to Warrington in 1946 as their No. 27. It was withdrawn in 1971 and subsequently used as a service vehicle. It has subsequently been preserved in Warrington's maroon and white livery.

The new authority introduced a new livery layout and added a mustard band. Also new in 1957 were Northern Counties-bodied Leyland PD2/20s Nos 60/1, which are seen parked in the garage yard on 14 July 1979 having been withdrawn in 1977 and 1978 respectively.

The 1960s intake of buses comprised six MCCW-bodied Leyland PD2/30s in two batches of three. Number 63 is seen emerging from the old coal yard at Corporation Street in Preston on 20 June 1977. The yard had previously been used as a temporary bus station during the 1972 Guild. Number 63 had brought a private party to Preston in conjunction with Queen Elizabeth II's Silver Jubilee visit to the town.

Also seen on a private hire working in Preston is No. 65 of the second batch of three. It was photographed in Blackpool Road on 12 July 1978 passing Eldon Street Primary School. Numbers 63 and 65 were the last two survivors of the sextet and both were withdrawn in 1978.

The final half-cab buses purchased by Lytham Corporation were three Leyland PD2A/27s with Massey bodywork in 1964. Not unsurprisingly, these were the last of the type in the Fylde fleet and were withdrawn in 1981. Number 68 was photographed at the junction of St Alban's Road and St David's Road South in St Annes on 26 March 1975 on the jointly operated (with Blackpool Transport) service 11 from Lytham to Blackpool.

Number 69 of the same batch was photographed on Preston North End's car park on 10 May 1979 having worked a Troop Special to the nearby barracks on the occasion of Queen Elizabeth II's visit to Preston. Note the addition of a mustard band to the livery arrangement.

Bolton Corporation had latterly operated a large number of half-cab double-deckers which had mainly comprised Daimler CVGs and Leyland Titans, but all had been withdrawn from PSV use by Greater Manchester Transport (GMT) by 1975. On 22 March 1978, GMT ELC-bodied Leyland PD3/4 No. 6654 (ex-Bolton No. 154), which was new in 1961, was photographed in Deansgate in Bolton on driver tuition duties. Ironically, the car alongside is also a learner driver.

Also commandeered for the training fleet was former Bolton Corporation 1956 MCCW-bodied Leyland PD2/13 No. 77 (GMT No. 6577). This view was recorded in the Esplanade at Rochdale on 20 July 1976. Number 77 was saved for preservation and has been restored in the Bolton maroon and cream livery (see inset).

GMPTE also dispensed with Bury Corporation's former half-cab double-deckers at an early juncture of their modernisation plan. GMT No. 6389 was a 1967 ELC-bodied Leyland PD2/37 and had been No. 189 in the Corporation fleet. It was photographed in the Bury garage yard with two of Bury's trio of Daimler Roadliners, which were purchased in the same year, on 13 February 1976.

In 1958 Bury Corporation bought a batch of twenty Weymann-bodied Leyland PD3/6s numbered 201–20. They had rear entrances fitted with platform doors. The former No. 212 (GMT No. 6362) is seen alongside the garage in George Street on 9 March 1975, by then confined to driver tuition duties. No. 201 of the same batch is preserved.

Leigh Corporation latterly had a mixture of Leyland Titans and AEC Renowns, all of which were of a low-height configuration. Still wearing its SELNEC Southern emblem, 1957 ELC-bodied Leyland PD2/20 No. 6953 (ex-Leigh No. 53) is seen in Leigh bus station on 18 September 1974. This was one of a pair purchased that year. The bus station was rebuilt/remodelled in 1992.

Number 6937 (ex-Leigh No. 37) was a 1962 ELC-bodied Leyland PD3A/3. It was photographed in Manchester Road at Walkden on 27 January 1977 whilst working on loan to LUT's Swinton garage on local service 31 to Mount Skip. Passing is LUT 1964 Northern Counties-bodied Guy Arab V No. 161 on service 12 from Bolton to Salford. The brick buildings behind were still standing in 2023.

On the same day another Leigh Corporation bus was seen somewhat distant from its home territory. ELC-bodied AEC Renown No. 6934 (ex-Leigh No. 34), new in 1964, was photographed parked up in Lloyd Road at Levenshulme. The scene was much the same in 2023, although the pavement island had been removed.

ELC-bodied AEC Renown No. 6929 (ex-Leigh No. 29) was a solitary bus purchased by Leigh Corporation in 1967 and was the last half-cab to join the fleet. On a warm May day in 1977 it was waiting to depart Warrington's Arpley bus station with a service for Leigh.

Another scene at Leigh bus station sees 1964 ELC-bodied AEC Renown No. 6908 (ex-Leigh No. 8) on 20 November 1975 waiting to depart on a local service. Two well-known destinations of the local Leigh services were 'Dangerous Corner' and 'Plank Lane'. Alongside is 1957 ELC-bodied Leyland PD2/30 No. 6959 (ex-Leigh No. 59).

A. Mayne & Son first started operating AEC Regent half-cab double-deckers in 1934. The operator had long been a thorn in the side of Manchester Corporation and its successors and habitually refused to sell out. Eleven Regent Vs joined the fleet between 1957 and 1965 and these provided the backbone of the service on route 46/213 which commenced at Stevenson Square. They continued in service until the late 1970s with registration No. 8860 VR the last survivor. Now preserved it is seen at Heaton Park on 2 September 1984.

On the formation of SELNEC Manchester Corporation was still operating a large number of half-cab buses virtually all of which were Daimler CVGs and Leyland PD2s; the Corporation never operated any PD3s. MCCW-bodied Leyland PD2/40 No. 3549, which was new in 1958, is seen turning out of Aytoun Street at Piccadilly on 20 July 1976. It is not displaying a depot code but was probably working off Princess Street garage (PS).

Similar bus No. 3557, along with newer version PD2/37 No. 3710 of 1964, are seen parked up on spare ground at Old Trafford on 4 August 1976. The latter was one of the last Titans to join the fleet before the operator turned to rear-engined buses for its requirements.

Number 3660 (TV18) was a 1961 MCCW-bodied Leyland PD2/37 whilst No. 3491 was a PD2/40 which was new in 1958 and carried a Burlingham-built body. By 1976 both buses had been placed in the Driver Training Pool and are seen in the yard at Hyde Road garage on 1 August.

Between November 1976 and February 1977 five former Manchester PD2/40s were amongst a number of buses loaned to Swinton LUT garage to cover vehicle shortages. Number 3524 was photographed in Bolton Road at Walkden on 27 January 1977 having arrived on a service 542 duty from Bolton.

One of the oldest former Manchester buses still running in 1975 was this MCCW-bodied Leyland PD2/12 working off Queens Road garage. Number 3443 was one of sixty of the type taken into stock in 1956 and is seen in Corporation Street near Victoria working a peak-time extra on 18 January. Whilst the Corn Exchange building (left of the bus) still stands the other buildings on either side of the road have been replaced.

The last batch of PD2 half-cabs bought by Manchester was Nos 3696–3720 in 1964. The former Corporation buses retained the same fleet numbers in the PTE fleet. Number 3713 is seen in Parker Street at Piccadilly on 4 May 1976.

Number 3516 was one of a small batch of Burlingham-bodied Leyland PD2/34s (pneumocyclic self-changing gears) which joined the fleet in 1958. Also photographed on 4 May 1976, it was laying over in Lever Street, off Piccadilly. The Royal George was trading as Nupas/Bella Spar in 2022.

Another of the 1964 MCCW-bodied Leyland PD2/37s, No. 3699, is seen in Moseley Street at Piccadilly on 22 March 1978. Following the construction and opening of the Manchester Metrolink in 1992 the arrangements for the local buses, now provided by a number of different operators, has changed significantly.

New in 1963, MCCW-bodied Daimler CVG6K (K = Kirkstall rear axle) No. 4642 was photographed turning out of Aytoun Street into Piccadilly on 8 May 1976. This is now the route of the Metrolink to Piccadilly station. The Grand on the left, which dates from the 1860s and is a listed building, has been refurbished with individual living apartments.

Number 4567 was a 1957 Burlingham-bodied Daimler CVG5K and is seen in Warrington Street in Ashton-under-Lyne on 18 September 1974 heading for Stevenson Square in Manchester. The Wooden Spoon was a well-known establishment in Ashton and was demolished in the late 1970s. Note the lady on the pavement taking a tumble.

The conductor stands alongside his charge, 1958 MCCW-bodied Leyland PD2/40 No. 3539, in Stevenson Square on 4 May 1976. There is still a bus stop at this location but it is no longer a terminus. The 181 would take No. 3539 along Oldham Road to nearby Chadderton. The route still operated in 2022 but terminated at Shaw Wren's Nest. The building behind has since been refurbished.

By the mid-1970s Manchester's half-cab/back loaders tended to supplement regular services at peak times. MCCW-bodied Daimler CVG6K No. 4648 was based at Northenden garage and was working a south Manchester limited-stop service from Piccadilly on 4 May 1976.

The long, enclosed bus shelters at Piccadilly disappeared many years ago. Similar bus No. 4639 is seen on the 259 stand waiting to depart for Davyhulme on 19 July 1977. Behind is similar-bodied Leyland PD2/37 No. 3707, which will be heading in much the same direction on service 263 to Barton.

Another view of Corporation Street sees 1958 Burlingham-bodied Leyland PD2/40 No. 3506 heading back empty to Queens Road garage on 7 May 1976. On the left is the Manchester Arndale Shopping Centre which had only opened the year before. Following a terrorist attack in 1996 the centre was completely refurbished and rebuilt over a ten-year period, which saw the buses that used the Arndale bus station moved to a new bus station at nearby Shudehill.

The North Western Roadcar (NWRCC) fleet was disbanded in January 1972 with some of its services and buses absorbed by the PTE, with the remainder passing to Crosville and Trent Motor Services. The PTE acquired the garages at Altrincham, Glossop, Oldham, Stockport and Urmston. Service 125 was a long-standing former North Western route from Glossop to Manchester via Hyde and is seen here being worked by former NWRCC Park Royal-bodied AEC Renown No. 1917 on 4 May 1976.

Rochdale Corporation bought forty Weymann-bodied AEC Regent Vs in 1956 followed by another eleven in 1957 to replace its ageing fleet of pre-war Daimler CWs and Leyland TDs. Number 6172 (ex-Rochdale No. 272) was photographed in the Esplanade on 13 February 1976. Turf Hill is a local district to the east of Rochdale town centre.

One more followed in 1958 and three more in 1959 which were fitted with rear-platform doors. Number 6219 (ex-Rochdale No. 319) was the sole acquisition in 1958 and is seen in the garage yard on 27 April 1975. The last of the type were withdrawn in 1977.

After a break of not ordering any new buses for ten years Salford City Transport received thirty-five MCCW-bodied Daimler CVG6s in 1962. These were followed by 103 similarly bodied Leyland PD2/40s from 1963–7. GMT Daimler CVG6 No. 4009, former Salford No. 120, was photographed departing Victoria bus station on 13 December 1975 bound for Weaste Lane.

Victoria bus station was situated right on the city boundary with Manchester. It was opened in December 1937 and closed in 1986 (it reopened for a short period in the 1990s during the construction of Shudehill). Former Salford CT 1967 MCCW-bodied Leyland PD2/40 No. 266 (GMT No. 3112) is seen on the stand for Agecroft on 13 December 1975. Above the wall is the approach road to Manchester Exchange station (closed in 1969).

One of Salford's most prestigious routes was the jointly operated service 8 to Bolton; a route which was still operated in 2022 by Diamond Bus Northwest. MCCW-bodied Leyland PD2/40 No. 3116 (ex-Salford No. 270), of 1967, is seen in Bolton's Moor Lane bus station on 22 March 1978. Behind is MCW Scania No. 1432 on the Trans Lancs Express to Stockport.

Another former Salford PD2 transferred away from its depot of origin was No. 3049 (ex-Salford No. 200), which is seen at Hyde Road garage on 9 November 1980. Along with the ex-Stockport PD2s and PD3s the former Salford PD2s were some of the last half-cab buses to remain in service with GMT. Part of Hyde Road garage was still in use by Stagecoach Manchester in 2022.

Another former Salford Leyland PD2/40 is seen at the Peel Green terminus of service 66 in New Lane Salford on 27 March 1978. Still on home territory, GMT No. 3080 was new to Salford as No. 234 in 1966. This bus stop was still served by service 66 in 2022, which was then operated by Diamond Bus Northwest between Eccles and Prestwich.

The SHMD Board favoured Daimler buses for many years and in 1964 added a batch of six CVG6s to its fleet. Based in Stalybridge, the Board operated services in the surrounding area of Hyde and Dukinfield and to Manchester. Number 5609 (ex-SHMD No. 9) was photographed in Ashton-under-Lyne bus station on 13 February 1976. Thereafter the operator bought rear-engined buses.

The year 1958 had seen the Board's first deviation from Daimler double-deckers for many years when eight Northern Counties-bodied Leyland PD2/40s were purchased. Number 5691 (ex-SHMD No. 91) is seen in the garage yard at Ashton on 27 April 1975.

Stockport Corporation purchased its first Leyland Titan PD2s in 1949. These were interspersed with Crossley's DD42 model. Such was Stockport's allegiance to Leyland that the authority continued to purchase half-cab Titans until the end of production in 1969. On 16 August 1979 three of Stockport's ELC-bodied Titans, GMT Nos 5861/71/77, are encapsulated in the same shot at Piccadilly Gardens. Service 192 to Hazel Grove ran at very frequent intervals and was still operated to a prolific timetable by Stagecoach in 2023.

Former Stockport Corporation 1963 ELC-bodied Leyland PD2A/30 No. 5806 (ex-Stockport No. 6) was photographed in Queen Street in Farnworth on 27 January 1977 whilst working on loan to LUT. The service was route 20, which ran from Farnworth to Hollins Green.

The last half-cabs purchased by Stockport were twelve ELC-bodied Leyland PD3/14s in 1969, six of which had open-platform rear entrances and six of which had doored front entrances. Number 5897 (ex-Stockport No. 97) was one of the latter and is seen in Stockport's Mersey Square on 16 August 1979.

No. 5833 (ex-Stockport No. 33), which was new in 1965, was photographed in Dialstone Lane on 19 July 1977 working out of Stockport on a local service to Stepping Hill. In 2022 Dialstone Lane was served by service 375, which operated out to Mellor.

Stockport Corporation buses had latterly been painted in an attractive crimson and cream livery. 1962 ELC-bodied Leyland PD2A/30 No. 5961 (ex-Stockport No. 361) had somehow managed to escape a repaint and still retained the town coat of arms as late as September 1974 and is seen at Mersey Square. The journey out to Mellor (Longhurst Lane) via Marple is around 7½ miles.

Two of Stockport's ubiquitous ELC-bodied Leyland PD2/40s are seen parked on the Chestergate bus park on 19 July 1977. They are No. 5815 (ex-Stockport No. 15) of 1964 and No. 5826 (ex-Stockport No. 26) of 1965.

Two of the 1968 batch of ELC-bodied Leyland PD3/14s, Nos 5880/5 (ex-Stockport Nos 80/5) are also seen on the bus park on 16 August 1979. Even as late as this the operator still specified open rear entrances on their buses. This is now the site of Stockport bus station, which was opened in March 1981. The area was again redeveloped in the early 2020s.

ELC-bodied Leyland PD3/14 No. 5875 (ex-Stockport No. 75) was photographed in Buxton Road at Stepping Hill on 19 July 1977 working a duty on the long route from Manchester to Hazel Grove. This scene is near the junction of Bonis Crescent. The Nationwide Building Society is now a Papa Johns' pizza outlet.

In 1960 the municipality bought ten PD2/30s with rear-entrance sixty-seat bodies constructed by Longwell Green Coachworks of Bristol. These were numbered 343–52. The distinctive shape of the former No. 348 (GMT No. 5948) is seen in Mersey Square on 19 July 1977 whilst in use as a driver tuition vehicle.

Wigan Corporation remained a separate municipal operator until 1 April 1974 when it was absorbed by the Greater Manchester PTE. A staunch supporter of both local coach-building firms, these two Leyland PD3A/2s represented their loyalty as No. 3240 (formerly Wigan No. 71) was bodied by Northern Counties and No. 3236 (39) carried a Massey Brothers' body. They were photographed on the central bus park on 3 January 1977.

The Wigan Corporation livery was a sparkling wine red and white applied in an attractive arrangement. GMT No. 3230 (57) was repainted as such and is also seen on the town centre bus park on 25 June 1977. The two lights either side of the destination box were illuminated green at night to distinguish the buses from local rival Ribble.

Although working a local Manchester service to Clayton Bridge, GMT No. 3276 (11) was still displaying a WN garage code when it was photographed at Piccadilly Gardens on 19 July 1977. Number 3270 was a Massey-bodied Leyland PD2A/27 and was new to Wigan Corporation in 1964 and was most probably working off Hyde Road garage.

Wigan purchased four Northern Counties-bodied Leyland PD2/37s with exposed radiators in 1967 with fleet numbers 72, 73, 78 and 113. The latter is seen in New Market Street in its home town on 25 June 1977. Market Street is in the background whilst The Galleries shopping centre (opened in 1989) has been built on the land occupied by the surface car park. Service 623 to Worsley Hall was previously numbered 23.

Some of the oldest former Wigan Corporation buses acquired by the PTE were a batch of ten Leyland PD3/2s which were bodied by both Massey and Northern Counties in 1959. Northern Counties-bodied No. 3209 (68) is seen in Wigan Wallgate on 25 June 1977. Coxons Opticians had become the Little Fifteen Eatery by 2022.

Similar bus No. 3207 (66) was photographed on the same day in the erstwhile Station Road in the town centre waiting to leave for Ashton-in-Makerfield. Behind is GMT No. 3333, a Northern Counties dual-door-bodied Leyland AN68/2R which was new to Wigan in 1972 as their No. 4. The Station Road area was extensively redeveloped in the 1980s.

GMT No. 3276 (11) is seen again in Station Road in Wigan just three weeks before it was photographed in Manchester, on 25 June 1977. Similar bus No. 3274 (150) is waiting behind. As can be seen from the original Wigan fleet numbers, the previous numbering system was somewhat haphazard. The Worsley Mesnes service had previously been numbered 10.

Greater Manchester Buses (GMB) acquired ten Routemasters in 1988 which were used on service 143 to West Didsbury along the busy Oxford Road corridor. They were given fleet numbers 2200–9. Number 2203 (the former LT RM1604) was photographed in Oxford Road on 19 August 1989. RM1604 passed to Rotherham & District in July 1990.

GMB No. 2209 was formerly LT RM1807. It was taken out of London service from Putney garage in October 1987 and acquired by GMB in August 1988. It was photographed in Piccadilly bus station on 12 October 1988. The venture was short-lived and RM1807 also passed to Rotherham & District in July 1990.

When Lancaster City Transport and Morecambe & Heysham Corporation merged on 1 April 1974 to form City of Lancaster Transport (CoL) both municipal operators' fleets contained an eclectic mix of half-cab buses. The Morecambe fleet contained twenty-four AEC Regent IIIs which had been new from the period 1949 to 1954. Number 68 was a Park Royal-bodied Regent III, new in 1950, which is seen in the garage yard at the Battery on 22 August 1975.

Seven of the 1949-built Regents were rebuilt as open-top buses in 1967/8. Number 60 was another Park Royal-bodied bus and is seen in Longlands Lane descending towards Heysham on 21 August 1976. It was renumbered in the CoL fleet as No. 589 and withdrawn in 1978.

In 1957 Lancaster City Transport purchased four Leyland-bodied PD2/41s, fleet numbers 128/9 and 881/2 – LCT used the registration numbers as fleet numbers. Now repainted into the CoL blue and white, No. 129 was photographed in Marine Road Central on 21 August 1976 heading for Heysham Harbour.

In 1951 Morecambe turned to Weymann for the bodywork on a batch of six Regents. Number 77 is seen parked in the garage yard on 10 August 1974. All the Regent IIIs originally had a separate route number box. This particular bus was withdrawn in 1975.

Following the creation of CoL the new operator acquired a number of second-hand buses including six East Lancashire-bodied Leyland PD3/6s from Burnley & Pendle JTC in 1974. Number 32 was photographed on Preston North End's car park on 17 December 1977 having worked a Football Special for an FA Cup Round 2 match against Wrexham, which was won by the away team by two goals to nil.

Morecambe also obtained some new half-cab buses in 1957 comprising three Massey-bodied AEC Regent Vs. Number 84 is seen in Euston Road in Morecambe on 27 May 1975 bound for the local district of Torrisholme; the Regent was withdrawn the following year.

In 1963 LCT purchased a trio of East Lancashire-bodied Leyland PD2/37s followed by a similar repeat order in 1965. Number 203 of the first batch is illuminated by the sun as it crosses Skerton Bridge on 21 August 1976. It was converted to an open-top bus in February 1977 and was withdrawn in 1980. Visible on the right is the corrugated roof of Lancaster's Ribble bus garage.

Another of the former Morecambe open-top Regent IIIs, No. 64, was photographed in Marine Road East at Bare on 9 May 1976. The route to Heysham would take the bus along the Promenade road.

Number 466 was one of three thirty-six-seat rear-entrance (it was later rebuilt to forward-entrance with thirty-five seats) Northern Counties-bodied Daimler CVG5s purchased by LCT in 1952. Whilst Nos 467/8 didn't survive beyond 1957, No. 466 passed to CoL and was kept for special use until 1978; it is now preserved. Number 466 was photographed outside Lancaster Castle Prison on 27 May 1975 on a duty it performed many times.

CoL also acquired four Massey-bodied Leyland PD2/30s from Maidstone Borough Transport in 1975. These were something of a stop-gap measure – they barely lasted in service for twelve months and were withdrawn still in Maidstone livery. Number 413 is seen at Heysham on 1 October 1975.

Lancashire United (LUT) was formed in December 1905 and first registered at an address in Liverpool. The principal depot was situated at Howe Bridge just outside Atherton where first trams, then trolleybuses and finally buses were garaged. LUT was a staunch supporter of Guy buses in the late 1950s and 1960s and bought them in large numbers. Northern Counties-bodied Guy Arab V No. 267 was photographed in Chorley Road at Swinton on 29 November 1975 having commenced its journey in Wigan.

In 1961 LUT broke with tradition and received ten Guy Arab IVs with MCCW bodies. Number 43 is seen outside the garage at Howe Bridge on 19 March 1976. This large bus garage was opened in 1928 and closed in February 1998. Whilst the other nine of the batch were sold for scrap, mainly in 1975, No. 43 was saved for preservation in 1977.

Number 218 was the first of twenty-three Northern Counties-bodied Guy Arab IVs which entered the fleet in 1966 and is seen in Greengate (opposite Victoria bus station) at Manchester on 29 December 1976. It remained in service until May 1978. The redundant railway bridge decking has since been removed and redevelopment has taken place on both sides. Some journeys on service 38 ran as far as Wigan.

Guy Arab V No. 287 was new to LUT in November 1967 and was one of the last half-cabs to be purchased. This was the terminus of service 1, which was jointly operated with Merseyside PTE (originally St Helens Corporation) and ran between Atherton and St Helens. The Asia Kitchen shop had been rebranded as the Jigsaw Sandwich Bar by 2022 and all the chimney pots had disappeared from the terraced houses.

Guy Arab V No. 136 was the odd one out of a batch of seventeen buses purchased in 1963; the other sixteen had rear open entrances as opposed to a front-doored entrance. Number 136 has stopped for a crew change at Howe Bridge and is being overtaken by Plaxton-bodied Seddon 'Pennine' RU No. 342 on 20 November 1975. The suspended cradle is a remnant from the long-closed Howe Bridge Colliery.

Guy Arab V No. 195, new in 1965, was photographed in Market Street at Farnworth on 29 November 1975 on the relatively short route (5)43 from Bolton. LUT services were renumbered into the GMT series in 1974. On 1 January 1976 LUT became a wholly owned subsidiary of GM Transport, but was not fully absorbed until 1 April 1981.

A view inside Atherton garage recorded on 20 November 1975. Heading the two lines of buses are rear-entrance Northern Counties-bodied Guy Arab IV No. 53 and Guy Arab V No. 134. Around half the fleet was garaged at this large depot. The former SLT trolleybus depot on the opposite side of the road had been converted to a bus overhaul works. The last half-cabs in the fleet were withdrawn in December 1980.

Former Birkenhead Corporation Massey-bodied Leyland PD2/40, Merseyside PTE No. 61 (renumbered from No. 131), was photographed in Baldwin Street in St Helens town centre on 25 June 1977. This was one of a batch of fifteen Titans bought by Birkenhead in 1966.

Two more former Birkenhead Corporation Massey-bodied Leyland PD2/40s, Nos L460/1 (formerly Nos 88 and 85) are seen parked in the garage yard at Seaview Road in Liscard on Wallasey on 1 May 1976. These were part of another order received in 1963. Seaview Road garage was closed by the PTE in 1986 and the site has since been redeveloped.

Birkenhead Corporation bought 149 Leyland Titan PD2s, all with Massey bodies, between 1957 and 1967 and mostly in batches of fifteen. No. 70 was new in 1962 and is seen parked at the Seacombe bus station/Mersey Ferry Terminal on 23 July 1974. It is painted in the Wirral version of the PTE colours. The buildings behind had only recently been demolished.

Number 142 was one of the last fifteen back-loaders delivered to Birkenhead Corporation in 1967. Along with Wallasey Corporation the operator became part of the Merseyside PTE in December 1969. These were some of the last half-cabs in the PTE fleet. A 1962 example, No. 71, is parked behind – the location is Derby Square in Liverpool city centre as seen on 1 May 1976. Extensive investment and redevelopment work in the area has taken place in the following forty-odd years.

St Helens and Southport corporations both joined the Merseyside PTE on 1 April 1974. The former had a significant number of half-cab buses in the fleet comprising PD2As and Regent Vs. Leyland PD2A/30 No. 21 (originally L21) was new in 1962 and carried a MCCW body. It is seen in Ellamsbridge Road in St Helens on 25 June 1977. The school building behind has since been demolished and replaced by housing.

Number 38 (L38) was a 1962 MCCW-bodied AEC Regent V. It is depicted at the terminus of service 97 in Cross Lane in Prescot on 25 June 1977; behind is Saunders Avenue. In 2022 this stop was served by Arriva service 297, which ran from St Helens to Kirkby.

St Helens Corporation had two bus garages, one at Hall Street in the town centre and one in Jackson Street (previously known as Langtree Street). The latter was opened in 1947 and is where MCCW-bodied Leyland PD2A/30 No. 22 (L22) was photographed on 18 February 1978. The gas holder is no longer there but the garage was still in use by Arriva in 2023.

The last batch of half-cabs to join the St Helens fleet consisted of six Leyland Titans and three Regent Vs in 1967. East Lancs-bodied Leyland PD2A/27 No. 55 is seen in Warrington Road in Prescot on 25 June 1977. Most of the former St Helens half-cabs stayed local to the town during their PTE days with the last of the type being withdrawn in 1979.

Liverpool Corporation bought vast numbers of PD2s and Regent Vs in the late 1950s. Number L303 was a Leyland PD2/30, one of a batch of thirty completed by MCCW in 1961 (originally placed with Crossley). It is seen alongside the Royal Liver Building in Water Street on 23 July 1974. A number of Liverpool buses were unpainted.

Southport Corporation purchased twelve Leyland-bodied PD2/3s in 1947, six of which were converted to open-top buses in 1962/3. Whilst Nos 85/8/9 had all been withdrawn by 1974, Nos 84/6/7 became Nos 184/6/7 in the PTE fleet. Flanked by the other two, No. 184 is seen inside Southport's Canning Road garage on 27 May 1975. The garage was still in use by Arriva Buses in 2023.

Number L472 had previously been Southport Corporation No. 39, one of five Weymann-bodied Leyland PD2/20s purchased by the Corporation in 1957. It is seen in the former Liverpool Corporation garage yard at Green Lane on 30 August 1976.

Southport bought three batches of four Weymann-bodied Leyland PD2/40s in 1961/2/5. Number 48 of the second batch is seen in St Nicholas Place near Liverpool Pier Head on 19 March 1976 on a special service.

In 1963 Southport Corporation took the unusual step of acquiring three Burlingham-bodied Leyland PS2/5s from Ribble Motors and converted them to open-top buses. Number 11, formerly Ribble No. 242, was parked opposite the war memorial in London Street on 18 August 1974. The branch of the NatWest Bank was still open for business in 2022.

Number 10, formerly Ribble No. 240, was later converted into a towing vehicle. It is seen alongside the garage in Cobden Road on 18 July 1980. The third of the trio, No. 12, has been privately preserved.

The PS2s were replaced by PD2 open-top conversions in the mid-1970s. Southport No. 53 had been new in 1965. Now renumbered to 0053, it is seen in Eastbank Street on 15 August 1982. Numbers 51/4 of the same batch, along with No. 58 of the 1967 MCCW-bodied batch, were also converted to open-top format.

For twenty years, between 1946 and 1965, Preston Corporation purchased a succession of Leyland Titans from PD1s through to PD3s. MCCW-bodied No. 64 was one of a batch of seven that entered service on 1 January 1959. It is seen outside Saul Street swimming baths on 18 November 1978 on a 'Baths Special'. This was its last day in service.

Seven more of the type were purchased in 1961 and entered service towards the end of September. No. 14 was on a 'Hospital Special' when photographed outside the Continuation Hospital in Midgery Lane on 23 September 1979. This working had a seventy-minute layover at its destination.

Preston's next acquisitions were a further seven MCCW-bodied Leyland PD3A/1s with the 'St Helens' front in 1963. Number 84 was photographed in Fylde Street on 27 November 1976. This route still runs as service 23 to Fulwood's Asda. The building has since been replaced by new university buildings and the whole area has been transformed beyond recognition.

One of Preston's PD3 'rebuilds' is seen parked in Parkside on 9 September 1978 on 'Football Special' duty. No. 2 entered service on 24 July 1961 and was withdrawn on 31 March 1979. It is now preserved. The match was an old League Division 2 game between Preston and Millwall which ended scoreless.

Four of the highbridge buses were also rebuilt as PD3s. No. 50 entered service as such on 13 December 1962 and was withdrawn on 31 January 1978. In this view, recorded on 2 August 1974, it is depicted in Adelphi Street returning from Queens Drive. It is in the livery style used by the Corporation from January 1967 to November 1973, the buses having previously been painted maroon and cream.

Freshly out of the paint shop, 1961 MCCW-bodied Leyland PD3/4 No. 15 is seen providing work's transport for Peter Craig's Mail Order Co. in Balcarres Road on 19 May 1977. Three of this batch, No. 15 included, gave the council nearly twenty years of service.

A new docking shop was created in part of No. 1 garage in 1965 and 1963 MCCW-bodied Leyland PD3A/1 No. 70 was photographed over the pits on 13 January 1980. This was the last half-cab bus to remain in service with the authority and was withdrawn on 1 November 1981. Its final resting place was in the scrapyard of G. Jones at Barnsley.

In 1954 the Corporation bought a batch of eight highbridge and two lowbridge Leyland PD2/10s – the latter were later rebuilt as PD3s. No. 57 was photographed in Barry Avenue on the Ingol estate on 18 June 1974 working a duty on the jointly operated (with Ribble) P4 service. Number 57 was withdrawn in January 1976 and converted for use as a driver training vehicle.

The only exceptions to Preston's double-deck post-war purchases before 1968 were two ELC-bodied Leyland PS1s, which entered service on 1 June 1949. They had little regular work after 1954 but remained in service until December 1968. Number 74 is seen inside the garage on 20 September 1976, having latterly been used as a mobile polling station. Both the PS1s are now preserved.

In 1956/7 the Corporation purchased eighteen Crossley-bodied Leyland PD2/10s. These entered service over a protracted period. Number 31 is seen at the Adelphi roundabout (now completely remodelled and known as University Square) with a service for Fulwood Queens Drive on 11 August 1976. It was the last rear-entrance bus to remain in service with the undertaking and was withdrawn on 7 October 1976.

Prior to the Crossleys, the Corporation bought a small batch of five MCCW-bodied Leyland PD2/10s in 1955; they entered service on 1 November. Number 83 was photographed in a deserted Fishergate on 25 August 1976 heading out to Hutton on the jointly operated P5 service. The branch of the NatWest Bank on the right was the subject of an armed raid in broad daylight on 18 September 1988; the bank manager and his daughter had been kidnapped to facilitate the robbery. It is no longer a bank.

Another joint route was the P2, which ran from the Plough Inn at Penwortham to Fulwood Lightfoot Lane. Wholly operated by Ribble for thirty years, the route was split in April 1978, with Preston operating the northern section. 1965 MCCW-bodied Leyland PD3A/1 No. 72 departs a snowy bus station on 21 January 1979 with a backdrop of Leyland Panthers.

One of the 1963 batch of Titans, No. 85, was photographed in Friargate whilst crossing the junction of Ring Way on 25 June 1974. Buses were rerouted away from the upper section of Friargate way back in early 1991. Number 85 was withdrawn in March 1980 and was bought by Geoff Lister (dealer) of Bolton.

This former Rawtenstall Corporation Leyland PS2/1 was one of a pair that were bought in 1950 and originally carried a rear-entrance body. Built by East Lancs, it was rebuilt to front entrance in 1962. No longer in use as a PSV, it was photographed inside the Rossendale Borough garage on 5 October 1980, equipped as a towing vehicle. It is now preserved.

Rawtenstall Corporation bought four ELC-bodied Leyland PD3/4s in 1964 followed by four more in both 1965 and 1966. These were all seventy-three-seat front-entrance buses. Number 31, of the first batch, is seen waiting to depart the Bacup Road bus stop for Bacup on 12 May 1975. Note the simple destination with no service number shown.

Haslingden Corporation merged with Rawtenstall in April 1968 to form Rossendale JTC. ELC-bodied Leyland PD2/40 No. 44, new in 1960, had been No. 14 in the Haslingden fleet. Number 44 was in use as a driver tuition vehicle when photographed inside the Rossendale garage on 5 October 1980. It was still in use in 1986.

Rossendale acquired two ELC-bodied PD3s from Haslingden Corporation. The former Haslingden No. 2 was a PD3/14 which was new in 1967 and took the number 46 in the merged fleet. It is seen working the free service to Rawtenstall's Asda on 22 April 1982 – this was the last year of operation for Rossendale's half-cabs.

Warrington Corporation was another North-West municipal operator that operated two small batches of Fodens after the war, interspersed with two batches of Bristol K6Gs. However, these were followed by the more traditional Leyland Titans. ELC-bodied Leyland PD2/40 No. 13 was captured in Hallfields Road at Westy on 18 February 1978. There is now a double mini-roundabout at this location.

After purchasing a batch of Daimler Fleetlines in 1963 the operator opted for more Leyland Titans in 1964/5. The last batch were classed as specials, being PD2/40s, which were only 7 feet 6 inches wide. Number 41 was parked in front of the garage workshops at Wilderspool on 18 February 1978. It is painted in the previous livery layout.

A combination of rear-entrance and forward-entrance PD2s are seen on the bus stands in Bridge Street on 6 May 1978. Both with ELC bodywork, No. 88 was new in 1962 whilst No. 52, behind, dated from 1965. Number 88 remained in service until 1980. Bridge Street is now pedestrianised and the buildings behind are Grade II listed.

The operator acquired two former Leicester City Transport ELC-bodied Leyland PD3/1s in March 1975; they had short careers with Warrington and were withdrawn after two years' service. Number 6 (ex-Leicester No. 206) was photographed in Runnymeade at Woolston on 19 March 1976. This is the junction of Manchester Road.

Two of Warrington's 'special' ELC-bodied Leyland PD2/40s, Nos 50 and 41, which are seen in Buttermarket Street on 21 May 1978. Number 50 was one of the last half-cabs in service and was withdrawn in 1981. Also on view is 1970 Seddon-bodied Bristol RESL No. 59. Warrington's buses were still owned by the council in 2023.

Another of the specials: No. 45 is seen at the terminus of service 1 in Cleveland Road at Orford. The bus would have next worked through to Westy. Although the bus stop still exists at this location (junction of Poplars Avenue), it is no longer a terminus.

Widnes Corporation was renamed Halton Borough Transport on 1 April 1974. At the time the fleet contained an assortment of Leyland Titan PD2s. Still displaying the old 'Corporation' name, 1961 ELC-bodied Leyland PD2/40 No. 33 was photographed in the Caldwell Road bus park on 25 October 1974.

Widnes Corporation also acquired a small number of PD2s from Wigan Corporation. Number 18 joined the fleet in 1972 and was a 1958 Massey-bodied Leyland PD2/10 which had been No. 9 in the Wigan fleet. It is seen in the bus park on the same day.

Crosville was a significant operator throughout Cheshire and North Wales and had several different marques of the prolific Bristol Lodekka amongst its ranks. The FL model was a 30-foot-long version first introduced in 1959. Numbers DFG242 and DFG63 are seen at Warrington's Arpley bus station on 21 May 1977.

The last model produced was the shorter (27-foot) FS version in 1960. Number DFG192 was photographed on the garage forecourt at Chester on 9 February 1975. Bristol-built Lodekkas were all sent to Eastern Coach Works factory at Lowestoft for bodying. Crosville's last half-cab Lodekkas were withdrawn in 1982.

Equally well known in the North West and beyond was the fleet of Ribble Motor Services. The last half-cab buses to join the fleet were a large batch of 120 MCCW and Burlingham-bodied Leyland PD2/12s and PD2/13s in 1955/6. The last of these were retired from passenger service in 1972. Preserved Burlingham-bodied Leyland PD2/12 No. 1455 was photographed on Central Beach at Lytham on 17 August 1997.

Four of the MCCW-bodied PD2/13s were converted to driver tuition vehicles in the early 1970s. Number 1392 was renumbered to TU1 for such duties and is seen at the top of Brockholes Brow in Preston on 17 July 1976.

Possibly the last half-cab bus in use with Ribble was this 1962 Alexander-bodied Albion Lowlander which began life as a demonstrator before working for Bamber Bridge Motor Services. It was acquired by Ribble (numbered 1968 and with a modified destination screen), along with BBMS in April 1967 and latterly worked off Wigan garage. It is seen in Morecambe garage yard on 1 October 1975, having run its last mile for Ribble.

Lofty's Tours commenced operations in 1967 from a base in Mickle Trafford near Chester. Predominantly a coach operator these four MPTE (former Birkenhead Nos 151–4) 1967 Massey-bodied Leyland PD2/37s were acquired for school contract work in 1977. They were photographed in the depot yard on 1 September. Lofty's ceased trading in 2008. Number 152 is now preserved.

J. Fishwick & Sons was founded in 1907 but ceased trading in 2015. One of their principal routes was between Leyland and Preston, which for many years required the use of lowbridge buses owing to a railway bridge with restricted headroom at Penwortham. Latterly Fishwick had operated a number of Weymann-bodied PD2/40s. Seen at the Fishwick garage on 28 September 1997 is the by then privately owned No. 5 alongside ECW-bodied AN69/1R No. 23.

Another long-standing independent operator in Lancashire is Holmeswood Coaches of Rufford. Holmeswood was founded in 1947 and have operated school contract services for many years. In 1974 former Ribble 1956 Burlingham-bodied Leyland PD2/12, latterly No. 1434, was amongst their ranks and was photographed at the garage on 25 October.

On 27 January 1977 this collection of second-hand half-cab buses was to be found in Holmeswood's garage yard. They comprise former Lothian Buses MCCW-bodied Leyland PD2/20 No. 560, Alexander-bodied Leyland PD2/30 Nos 604/49 and former LUT Northern Counties-bodied Guy Arab IV No. 66.

Holmeswood's affinity to former Edinburgh municipal buses continued when they acquired this 1964 Alexander-bodied Leyland PD3/6, ex-Lothian No. 672. It was photographed on Preston North End's car park on 4 May 1979 in connection with an unrecorded event.

Lonsdales Coaches of Heysham had a long-standing contract to provide transport to and from the nearby nuclear power station construction sites. For this purpose, they acquired a varied selection of mainly half-cab double-deck buses. Seen in the garage yard on 1 October 1975 are former Great Yarmouth Corporation 1957 Massey-bodied Leyland PD2/22 No. 35 and former Colchester Corporation 1960 Massey-bodied Leyland PD2/31 No. 27.

Six years later and the buses in use on the contract had changed. This line-up, captured on 21 June 1981, comprised former Lothian Buses Alexander-bodied Leyland PD3/6s Nos 659/54/52 and former Preston Borough MCCW-bodied Leyland PD3A/1s Nos 71/3. Still in original fleet colours are former Lancaster PD2 No. 204 and Lothian PD3 No. 658.